THE BEATS OF A WILD HEART

by

Annette King (signature)

Annette M King

photos by

C. Greg Silva

(Unless specified otherwise)

"With every beat of my heart, I stand for Nature's children"

All poems in this book are original works by Annette M. King

Welcome to a brief journey into my wild heart through a few of my favorite images and words that often have been my way of sharing my inner thoughts, love and sometimes my frustration. My devotion to this mission and these animals is very real, and there isn't much I haven't suffered to be able to care for them. I work from a strong belief that they feel pain, cold, thirst, hunger, abandonment and fear much the way we do. My daily mission is to tend their needs with loving hands in a calm environment surrounded by the pure of heart and intent so that they may feel safe and thrive, and find their way back to their home, free of the confines of man, to pick up their lives in Nature once again.

"We all suffer the same"

Please enjoy these heartfelt poems that I have written over my two decades of caring for wildlife, and many of breathtaking images that Greg effortlessly produces with his lens, and thank you for your purchase that helps fund our most important and necessary work here at Wild Heart Ranch.

Annette King

I AM AN ANIMAL RESCUER

My job is to assist God's creatures
I was born with the need to fulfill their needs
I take in new family members without plan, thought, or selection
I have bought dog food with my last dime
I have patted a mangy head with a bare hand
I have hugged someone vicious and afraid
I have fallen in love a thousand times
and I have cried into the fur of a lifeless body

I have Animal Friends and friends who have animal friends
I don't often use the word "pet"
I notice those lost at the road side
And my heart aches
I will hand raise a field mouse
And make friends with a vulture
I know of no creature unworthy of my time

I want to live forever if there aren't animals in Heaven
But I believe there are
Why would God make something so perfect and leave it behind
We may be master of the animals,
But the animals have mastered themselves
Something people still haven't learned

War and Abuse makes me hurt for the world
But a rescue that makes the news gives me hope for mankind
We are a quiet but determined army
And making a difference ever day

There is nothing more necessary than warming an orphan
nothing more rewarding than saving a life
No higher recognition than watching them thrive
There is no greater joy than seeing a baby play
who only days ago, was too weak to eat

I am an Animal Rescuer
My work is never done,
My home is never quiet
My wallet is always empty
But my heart is always full

The above poem has circled the globe for many years. It has been changed, plagiarized and reprinted in many languages. I take no offense. It warms my heart to know that so many relate to my words, but this is the original and I can assure you, it was only inspired by my desire to get a group of wildlife rehabilitators to stop arguing amongst themselves and start supporting one another. It worked. ☺

Shooting Wildlife

There's more to me than fur
Which may come as a surprise
I know you'd see a spirit in me
If you looked into my eyes

My head is here to guide me
Not to decorate your wall
If you want to use a part of me
You had better need it all

There's more to me than beauty
I have a purpose and a will
I have responsibilities and things to do
That I must continue to fulfill

Your weapon, it may kill me
And my children and my mate
When I don't return with food tonight
You've sealed my family's fate

There's more to me than mystery
My life no different than you
I live to survive the best that I can
Hoping the day will see me through

So when you have me in your crosshairs
I ask, I beg, I pray...
Take only from me a photograph
And let me go about my way

The Hungry Horse

How cruel a world for those who trust
Who's gentle heart turns cold
When all is denied to nourish you
Leaving you weak and looking old

Once glory to sit upon your back
A gentle mouth took heed
They used you once upon a time
And now, deny your need

Your coat has lost its shimmer
Your bones tell us the tale
Your eyes once bright, are hollow
Your feet are long, your gums are pale

You stagger when you once could run
You move with arthritic pain
Your heart still beats, your mind still longs
For a fresh drink, for grass for grain.

I'm here to take you home with me
You will suffer never more
Green pasture and fresh water
And a barn for you in store

We will find your flesh returning
We will trim your teeth and feet
We will grain you every single day
All you care to eat

Someday when your body mends
And you are fit and fat and sound
I will sit with pride upon your back
And we will fly across the ground

For this that I am certain
though your world had fell apart
I can see through your shaggy coat and bones
to the starvation of your heart

My love will fill it up again
My care will make you strong
My hands will be on you every day
You are now wanted and belong

For every horse who has lived hungry
and for those who give relief
You couldn't be more supported
In this monumental grief

May your pastures grow green and free of thorns
and many blessings fill your day
May your bonds be tied with miracles
And all the hungry horses ride away

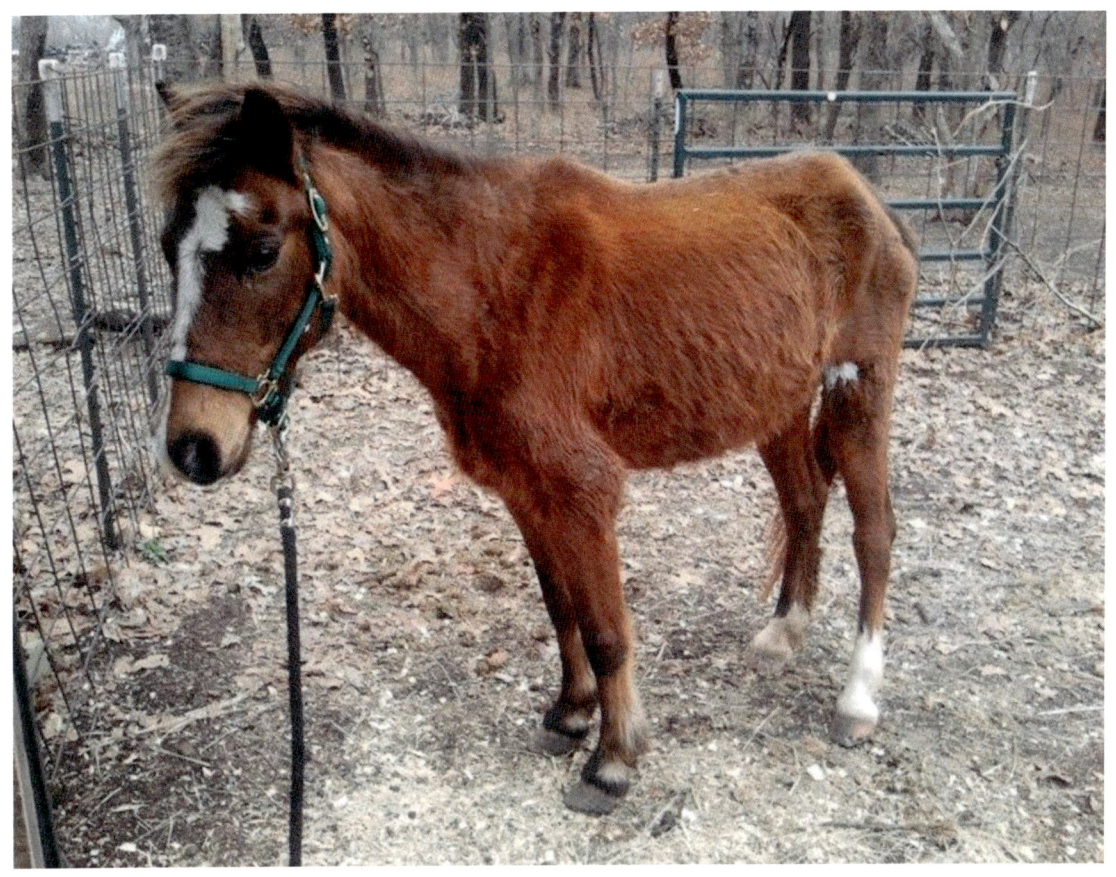

Photos by Annette King

We assumed Ginger was a baby when we brought her home. Too weak to stand, we stood her with an A frame and sling until she could hold her weight. Covered in rain rot and wounds from where the coyotes were trying to eat her, she had survived under three feet of snow while all of her pasture mates died of starvation, thirst and cold. A miracle that she survived at all.

Ginger a few months later. She actually was eighteen years old!

My Beloved Scars

I look down at my hands
There are more scars than skin
For some it might be unsightly
To me its where my memories begin

This one was from a bobcat
Who one day escaped from his cage
With no claws for him to hunt with
I caught him barehanded and felt his rage

These layers and layers of slices
From my hands all the way up my arm
Are hundreds and hundreds of raccoon kits
That scratched without meaning harm

Here was a baby black bear cub
Who was hungry beyond belief
He clung to my arm in a frenzy
'Til I learned welding gloves saved me that grief

This hole in my arm was a tree
That embedded its branch as I charged
Into the thick brush for a deer
That had just been hit by a car

And under the hair of my head
four slashes grooved into the bone

I was changing my cougar cub's bed
And she wouldn't leave mommy alone

But the scars that I cannot show you
The big ones that tore me apart
left behind from so many I've loved and then lost
Are the scars that once were my heart…

Photo of baby Kiara and I by Larry L Hagood
(rest in peace Daddy)

Lost Children of the Wild

They arrive in boxes and blankets and hands
Lost children of the wild
They are cold, hungry and missing their mom
Like any other displaced child

They have survived the unthinkable trauma
And they have found mercy with human care
They are brought to us each and every day
And they come from everywhere

We settle them in and get them warm
And give them everything they're needing
We tend their wounds and hunger
A constant marathon of feeding

Our wild ones are the treasures
Of a wilderness gone long before
They have adapted to our intrusion
And cannot avoid us anymore

It is our duty to provide
A place where they can grow
For "Nature taking its place"
Was lost to people long ago

So my thanks to those who take the time
To bring the baby that you found
To someone who knows just what to do
And will keep it safe and sound

And after dozens or hundreds of feedings
And long days and longer nights
Will release it back to where it belongs
And make our intrusion a little more right

Photo by Annette King

Have a Heart for the Wild

A heart for the wild beats strong inside of me
In every pair of frightened eyes I see my soul,
They arrive from everywhere, rescued with loving care
And have come into my hands to be made whole

Each spring and summer I feed babies who are orphaned
And injuries are cared for every day
At times a wild one will part, and it always breaks my heart
But I was here to care for them some final way

There are months as babies thrive while I'm exhausted
And times it feels my efforts are in vain
But when the day comes to let them go, In my heart I always know
They are worth every moment of my time and all the pain

For those who do not understand my mission;
Why choose a life that is so often tough?
I ask you see it through my eyes, these miracles in disguise
And that no matter what I give, its not enough

Our wild ones were here long before,
the people landed boats upon the shore
We survived upon their meat, having little else to eat
And now they don't hold value any more

So I ask how could we not provide them haven?
And I ask why we use them primarily for sport?
They spread the seeds that grow our trees and survive with distant ease
So why can we not give them our support?

They are never in our way, we are in theirs
Their patterns are all ancient and unchanged
They are going about their day, much the same in every way
It is us that invaded their home and rearranged

We owe them restitution for their space
At least some of what we have to help them grow
Hang a feeder in your yard when the weather makes it hard
For a bird to find a meal beneath the snow

There are not more wild animals than there used to be
They are simply running out of room to feed and hide
We have forced them from their home, having little space to roam
They forage, hunt and live now at our side

When trees are cut and roads and homes are built
And orphans are created for the loss
It is not "nature taking place", she didn't destroy anything for space
A rehabilitator will spend the time and pay the cost

So when you meet a squirrel that isn't quite afraid
Or raccoons and skunks move in to steal your feed
Respect their right to share your space, know they have evolved into this place
Because they sacrificed their homes to fill your need

"I see you!"

Here I Stand

Here I stand another day
An infection eating my withers away
Passers by don't seem to see
The sad and miserable state of me

I hang my head and stand in sorrow
Day after day and more tomorrow
Will anyone notice when I die?
Or will the ones who miss me be the flies?

Here I stand another day
My wound is clean and I have fresh hay
My doctor says I'm healing fine
That all I need is care and time

I wonder what they think of me
A skinny old horse is what some see
But there are more who see beyond my pain
My wound will heal, my weight will gain

I will stand another day
In a field of green, grazing away
Knowing all I need will never lack
And only the sun will be on my back

I will stand.

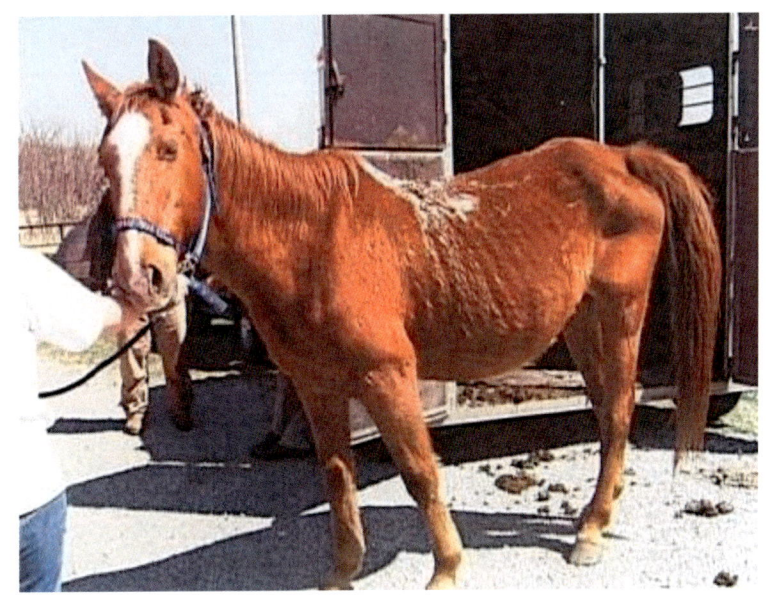

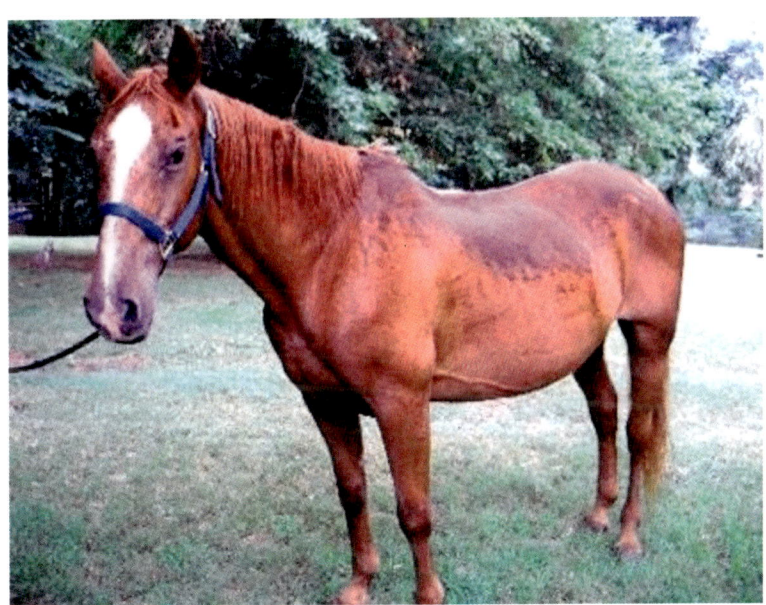

Photos by Annette King

Angels Have Paws

They often find me when my life has got me down
I have purpose when I know that they're around
In every pair of eyes, there's an angel in disguise
For the joy they bring makes it impossible to frown

Sometimes they know me better than I do
When I'm feeling a little sad, lonely and blue
They insist I stop to play, and my blues just fade away
And I'm thankful for a friend so smart and true

And when my little angels get old and gray
And their light on Earth begins to fade away
The hole within my heart is left gaping when they part
But they always seem to fill it with a stray

We say we care for them, but I know better
Every furry friend and bird of every feather
They come into our life, an end to loneliness and strife
Creating purpose, hope and memories we treasure

So when that aching need for a friend begins to smart
A purchase isn't where you need to start
A rescue is a place where an angel has a face
'Adoption' means "Chosen by the heart"

Now if you don't believe in Angels or their cause
I ask you reconsider and take pause
They are around us every day, disguised as lost or stray
And will find you not on wings, but tired paws.

The Christmas Tree

'Twas the night before Christmas and all through the wood
Not a creature was stirring, they were snuggled in good

The snow was now falling and the water was ice
But inside of the tree, it was warm, it was nice

Their mother had left for a late winter snack
and three little squirrels were waiting for her to come back

They snuggled and twitched, their tails kept them warm
As the wind started to blow with the cold winter's storm

The sun rose and it fell as the days came and went
The squirrels were now hungry, their food was all spent

They longed for their mother, they began to feel fear
Any minute they hoped she soon would appear

When outside the tree there arose such a clatter
Three babies emerged to see what was the matter

A man walking along with a dog at his side
It wasn't their mother so they scurried to hide

But with slippery ice and the wet winter snow
And the tree bough that rocked in the wind 'to and fro'

The squirrels lost their footing, they fell from the tree
And into the snow they plopped; "one, two and three!"

The man, he had seen them, he gathered his pup
And reached into the snow and gently scooped them all up

And into his jacket he wrapped the babies, so small
That fell from their nest in the tree, far too tall

And he knew at that moment he would not get his wood
The message from nature was much understood

She dropped in his path these babies just there
Who had long lost their mother and would die without care

So the woodsman he trudged up the hill in the snow
He could now see the smoke, not much further to go

Her cages were lined up and covered with care
Little creatures were healing and growing in there

He held out the bundle as she opened the door
He knew a warm bed and milk was in store

He left the wildlife rehabilitators home filled with glee
The spirit of Christmas he had found under a tree….

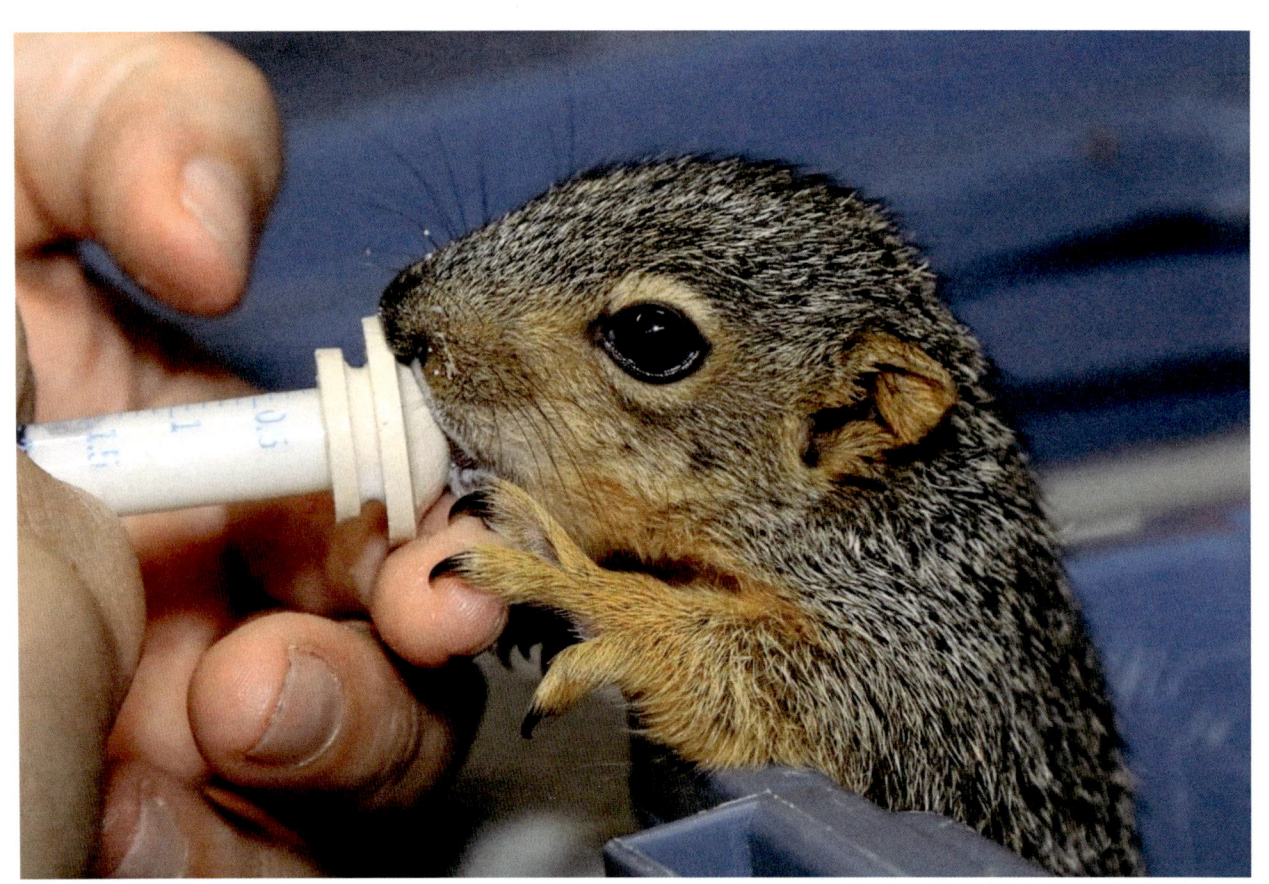

Photo by Annette King

Something Wild

Look into my eyes and you will see
Something you call wild
Though some would like to cuddle me
I am not a dog or cat or child

Finding food; my endless plight
I am created to survive
I roam the shadows of the night
And in the day I hide

I am not here to cause you grief
I have nowhere else to go
I don't mean to be a night time thief
It's the only way I know

So if you see me foraging
In places meant to feed another
The food I find is everything
For my sisters and my mother

Motion lights and things with sound
Will send us on our way
No need for harm this time around
Let us live free another day

Where the Nature Lives

Take me from the confines of walls

Into the shining sun

Away from the chaos of technology

Where a fawn has room to run

Where birds do not fear my presence

And water flows where it decides

Where the neighborhoods are underground

With little ones sleeping inside

Take me to the trees

Where I hear the whispers of the dawn

Where the land is scaped with deadfall

And no one has a lawn

Oh I want to live among this place

Where all is harmony

But that would end all that I love

Because the Nature doesn't want me

Waiting

I waited for you when you drove away
You patted my head and told me to stay
I watched as you disappeared over the road
I waited in darkness and huger and cold

I was waiting for you when the new people came
They took me and fed me and gave me a new name
I waited for you but knew you couldn't know
Where now to find me or where did I go

So I found a way out and I walked for so many days
And became just another of so many strays
And once again "rescued" on my quest I was found
I was warm I was fed but now locked in the pound

And all who walked past the bars to glance in my cage
Found me to thin or too scared, the wrong breed, the wrong age
Until finally one day my incarceration would end
Not because you had arrived or I'd found a new friend
All dogs go to Heaven, I now know this is true
And we will meet again,

I'll be waiting for you.

Photo by unknown

Little fawn so chewed and torn
Not yet a month since you were born
What's left of you will not repair
I feel your pain and your despair
I release you as I hold you near
From the earth you only suffered here
And in my mind you'll run away
Across heavenly fields you'll romp and play
And once again I'll shed a tear
Because you were loved your brief time here

"Are they still reading?" "Yeah I think so!"

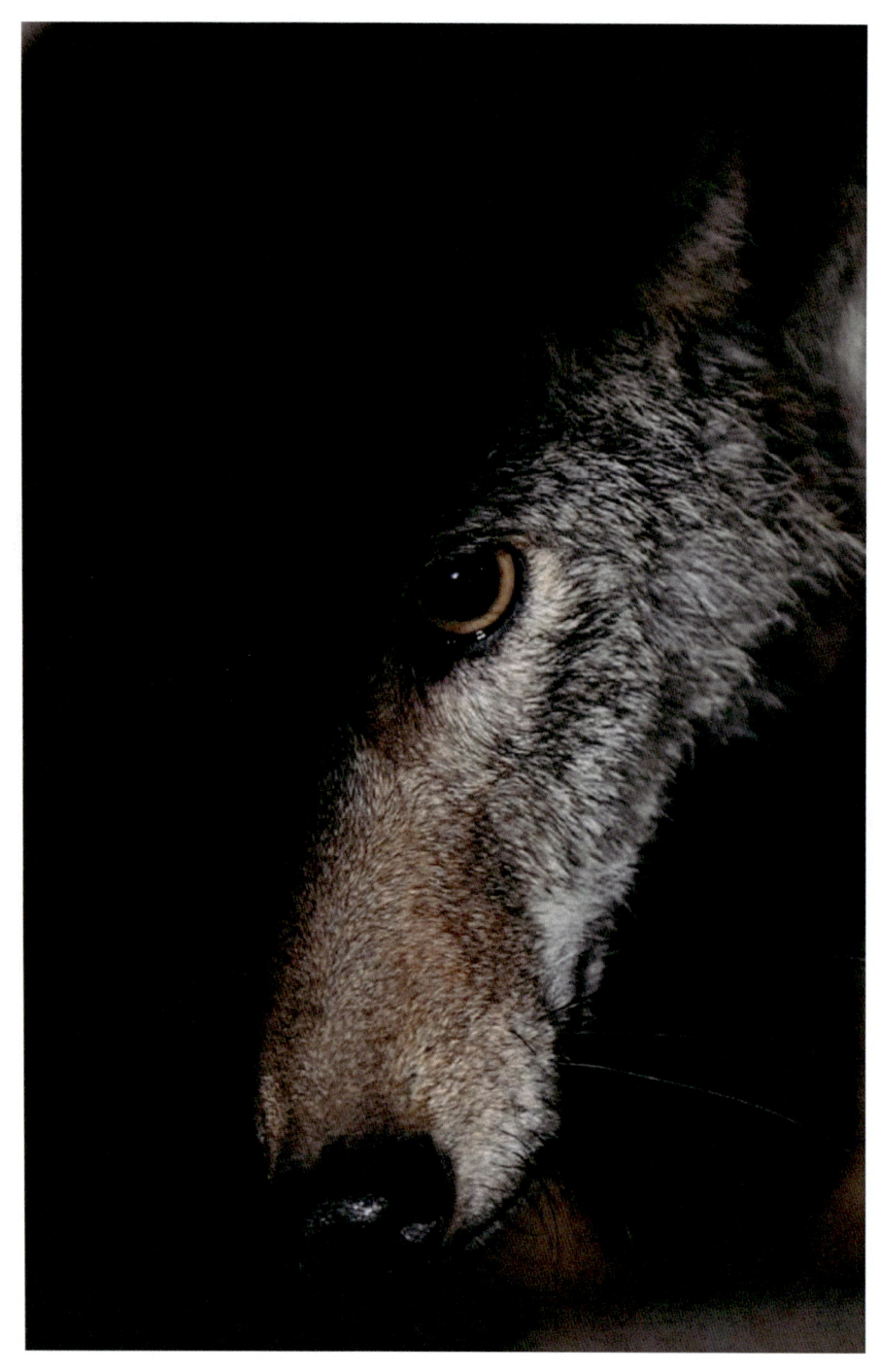

My daily battle

I want to work, I want to serve
I want to ease their pain
You kick me down but I come 'round
And get on my feet again

So come at me pain, with all you've got
I am ready and I'm able
To change the injustice that I can change
And serve the masters table

And with humble means I will not give up
Nor give in to a better place
There is no horror which can stop me
That I am unwilling to face

So take your best shot, give it all you've got
I mean what I have stated
I dare you pain, to break me
You can't beat the warrior you created

Dam Shame

Oh the mighty beaver man
Always doing what a beaver can
Busy building is what you do
All the day and night time too

Making sure you have a home
So your family doesn't have to roam
Making a pond where the water stays
To live out your happy beaver days

If only people could appreciate
The wonder Nature did create
In the amazing creature that is you
And all the awesome that you do

And now they say we made mistakes
To remove your kind from our streams and lakes
Because you cleaned what we pollute
And then we gave you all the boot

Now we suffer for our fail
Our hands need slapped with your mighty tail
For we have learned we needed you
That Nature always better knew

And every one of you I raise
Is welcomed on land where water strays
To build the fowl a place to nest
And put your fears finally to rest

Of course it's Bucky!

One of the hardest goodbyes ever before his release. I raised a strong and capable guy who today is doing his beaver thing with his mate in a beautiful and remote location where no one will ever harm him.

We Are All Broken

We are all broken in some big or small way
We all bare a scar that we hide every day
Some days it's hidden and some it will show
Some see it easily and some never know

We might limp a little or wear out too soon
We may fear loud noises or the size of a room
Or react with terror to something benign
Or lash out with anger at an inappropriate time

Sometimes its allergies, or a response to a smell
sometimes we live in an unexplainable hell
Often depression is the pit faced every day
Or anxiety robs many of their comfort to stray

Chronic nerve pain is a cross some people bare
Every movement they make causing pain they don't share
They don't want our pity or our constant concern
It's a life they must lead and they need us to learn;

That treatments are futile and nothing will cease
The pain that will haunt them and somedays increase
And helping them when they are determined to do
Might often be met with frustration toward you

We are all broken though the cause may be unclear
We are who we are, living in strength or in fear
And compassion and kindness and patience and care

Should be at the top of the list of the things that we share.

Because you never know how someone is broken or who
and the person who needs understanding might someday be you.

For all the broken people, including myself.

Believe

It is what you cannot see
And what somedays we feel
It's that voice within our heart
that gives us courage that is real

It's knowing we go on
When the body is void of life
It's the determination to push ahead
When all we meet is strife

It's the power we give our children
When they push out into the world
It's building every confidence
In a little boy or little girl

It is giving in to love
Knowing it will never take
The life you live and sacrifice
Will not be a mistake

It is taking thousands of wild animals
Without knowing if I can
Heal their wounds or raise them up
To be wild things again

But my sweet Mother always told me
"You can do anything you want to do,
you have many gifts, so use them
Because I believe in you"

Photo by Annette King

The Eyes of the Wild

I don't know how I got here
Or where my mother has gone
Everything sounds and smells so scary to me
I fear I won't live long

I feel your touch with gentle hands
You seem to care for me
I so want to know I'm safe again
Will you please set me free?

I have a life I need to live
But I'm not sure what to do
I am not supposed to be here
and I don't know if I can trust you.

———

Little one your eyes they tell me
That you are afraid of all you see
I have no way to tell you
That you are safe with me

I will feed you and I will give you care
To make you whole again
And every day I have to handle you
will be as briefly as I can

I respect your soul and all you are
that you are not my child
And for that I'll keep my distance
One day returning you to the wild.

The Beloved Old Soul

Your eyes they hold such wisdom
You've seen much throughout your years
You have stood strong in many a breaking storm
And held firm despite your fears

Your bones are aching in the winter
Your teeth are long, your back is swayed
You walk gingerly through pastures
Where the colt long ago had played

Many years ago that I abandoned
My place upon your back
You have earned your life of leisure
And there is nothing you will lack

But still so many ways I need you
Even though it will never be the same
I find my comfort in your sturdy grace
And cry my tears into your mane

How can I ever tell you
How much you will someday break my heart
Why can't you live forever
So that we will never have to part

But because of my great love for you
I will send you loping on ahead
And give you freedom from the body
And the amazing life we led

But know that my heart will follow
And will stay with you forever
So when one day I leave this place
We will be riding off together

Annette and Charley

The Creature

What is that hiding in the grass
Creeping slowly my direction
Is it a danger, does it mean harm
Or is it looking for affection

Closer and closer it doesn't stop
I freeze with utter fear
Up it comes to strike me down
And stops so very near

It makes a noise and a flash of light
And slithers from my space
My life is spared I have survived
Greg taking photos of my face!

Here I am to face another day
Of caring for those who were lost
Broken, sick or starving to death
They nearly paid the cost

Of being wild and living free
They have no owner to pay a bill
Just people who show up every day
To work from their own free will

We never know who will arrive
That may need a helping hand
Some will fight and injure us
But most will understand

That we are here to ease their pain
And get them on their feet
To release one day back to their home
And never again we meet

Why do we work so hard each day?
What burden do I blame?
Motivated by our empathy
"Because we all suffer the same"

The Vulture

Some may call you 'ugly'
Because they do not understand
Without you we would have a stinky home
With death littering the land

You circle a potential meal
Your brothers join the scout
Waiting to clean up what fails to live
Is what you are all about

You have a job that's like no other
And you thrive among the dead
Your mighty wings inspire awe
To make up for your funky head

And every time I see one of you
I smile to your kind
Thank you for cleaning up the mess
That so many leave behind

Another Turn..

In every turn of this rock we ride
We have a chance to change
Its merely a brief experience
That we can rearrange

Many of us are fortunate
We were born with our free will
We can choose for ourselves and those we love
Our destiny is ours we can fulfill

But yet we seem often to forget
How fortunate we are
To have a life we can fill with love
And do otherwise is so bizarre

Why would we seek to argue
To suffer and to fight
When life is what we make of it
We can live in darkness or spread the light

We are all victims of emotion
And we all hurt those that we treasure
But forging past our history
We can create a new forever

Let go of what torments you
And focus on what is good
Give the best of yourself to those who care
And forgive those that you should

The rock will turn and the sun will rise
Will you suffer again in sorrow?
Or reach to build a better you
To wake up as tomorrow

"Heidi" by Jeanine Montigue

Thank you for reading and supporting our wildlife!

Made in the USA
Coppell, TX
23 December 2020